Memory is that raccoon

Nolcha Fox

Acknowledgments

Thanks to these literary magazines for publishing my poems:

- A Thin Slice of Anxiety: "Electric Beater"

- Dark Entries: "Ashes"

- Diphthong Lit: "Stay as long as you want"

- Duck Head Journal: "Best Revenge," "Self-Portrait"

- Medusa's Kitchen: "A crazy idea," "A Little Less Enthusiasm, Please," "Best Revenge," "He climbed out," "Little lies," "Modern-day Eve," "Smoke," "Stay as long as you want," "Visiting Hours," "You Whisper"

- Lothlorien Poetry Journal: "Clouds blanket," "Enthusiasm without a plan"

- MiniMAG: "You're a poet, you see"

- Oneblackboylikethat Review: "Memory is that raccoon"

- Open Arts Forum: "Yes, I know I'm dying"

- Shooter Literary: "He took off his skin"

- Storyteller's Refrain: "Freeloader"

- The Gorko Gazette: "Cancer lives," "Stench, "You're Only Crazy"

- The Piker Press: "Give me that secret sauce," "I love you"

- Verse Virtual: "U-Turn"

- Whispers and Echoes: "Today is a dog," "Watch the day bruise"

- Alien Buddha Zine: "Little Black Dress," "Tulips," "My brain is stained," "The Incident"

- Five Fleas: "Death serves me," "You are a misguided," "Bed Head"

- Roi Fainéant Press" "Life in the Bathroom," "Love Is Blind (and Has a Stuffy Nose)"

- The Writers Club: "Glad you called," "See this"

Thanks to Sarah, Tony, and Tom for reading the first draft poems and cheering me on.

Thanks to my mother, who always believed I could write.

Contents

Love and Loss

A broken jar

to store the body of loss,
the coffee laced with sugar and shock,
the wrenched wild wings,
dried blood tears of sunsets past,
to leak the waning fading blue,
to hold what's left of you.

Ashes

Your urn isn't buried
very deep.
You easily reach up, knock
the stones off your marker,
to make a good seat
for smoking
that cigar I left you.
You inhale the ashes,
and return underground,
hoping I'll bring you
another cigar.

Believe

that to swallow something
beautiful is to keep it.
So, I swallow sunlight
resting on your ribs,
curved angel's wings
fluorescing this tiny
hidden hope that you
won't fly away.

Cancer lives

to eat.
It doesn't care
how much it weighs.
Cancer isn't a woman.
Obviously.

Death serves me

coffee and sits
at the table.
He points outside.
Those trees will
remain without you.
Want more cream?

Freeloader

In this tiny,
empty-of-you
room, I watch the
clock tick backwards.
Street-light only
on the block, all
the windows dark.
My eyes search
the gloom for the
wet halo of your hair
in sun, my nose
longs for the mint of
your laugh, my
body moves to the
sag where you once
slept beside me.
All of me reaches
to where you are
not. Your goneness
fills me. I should
charge you rent.

Glad you called

to say hello. It's been a while.
A year, you say. How are
the kids? I know you're only
filling time. Polite. What
do you really want?
I don't see them much.
They have their lives.
And you? What's going on?
The silence thick. The seconds
tick. Did I say something wrong?
Just want to hear your voice,
you say. Just want to know
that you're ok. Then silence.
You hang up.

He climbed out

of his pain when
no one was looking,
put pieces together
to make himself whole,
flew out of the embers,
a phoenix created
from fire and sorrow,
to ride the wind currents,
soar into the sun.

I love you

is a tea light
in a disposable
coffee cup,
a match tossed
into the ditch,
a rose on a coffin
lowered into dirt,
a lie you told me
last night.

If I open my mouth

will the dead crawl out,
leave me smaller
from their fleeing?
I carry them in
my cells, my breath.
But I am not their home.
Their hunger growls
to cross the seas,
return to ground
that birthed them.

Little Black Dress

I'll wear my little black dress,
the one you loved me in.
I'll walk down your street
like I own it,
the way you used to own me.

I'll wear my little black dress,
the one that made you crazy.
I'll walk down your street
like the last broad on earth,
and all the men are mine.

I don't care about you,
or what you say you'll do.
I'll wear that little black dress
like a second skin,
I'll wear it like my shroud.

Little lies

believe they are
invincible.
Little lies
believe they do
no harm.
They ignore
the warnings
posted round
the murky space
between us.
They jump in
and think
the water's fine.

Love is Blind (and Has a Stuffy Nose)

She reeked of debt, despair, and a litter box
that hadn't been cleaned for a week.
She bulged in all the wrong places.

He reeked of sweat, cheap cigars, and bad decisions.
Jowls hid his neck, a hat hid his bald spot.
He was wider than tall.

They both needed glasses and antihistamines.
They both wanted a bad drink and a good lay.
Or maybe it was the other way around.

Squinting through the smoky haze of a sleazy bar,
They saw in each other
the answer to their prayers.

Memory is that raccoon

I chased out of the trash cans
with a broom this morning.
It was collecting treasures
I don't know why I kept:
leftover pizza from
our first date
twenty years ago,
lightning bugs in a jar,
morning glories bursts
of purple on the fence,
snapdragons I made
to talk with stubby
toddler fingers,
sea shells from
a Mexican beach,
glass shards from
our first fight.

I thought if I tossed them out,
I'd have nothing
left to lose.

Offerings

He offers no acknowledgment
of her adoration. She only
wants a simple smile. She does
not see that he is empty. All he has
are his pretensions. He keeps them
for himself.

See this

ring. This promise. Broken.
Armor. Useless. See.
This ring. Twisting.
As you strike. The tree.
Twisted. Broken. Stump.
Useless. See. The rings.
Growth. Armor. You lied.
Again. You. Break.
Everything. You. Love.

Self-Portrait

I know I'm in your way,
a coat rack that you
blame for bruises,
a lampshade that you
bump at night.

I know that you don't
find me useful,
I know and yet I wait.
I wait and spill cream
on your sweater,
If you won't love me,
I'll take hate.

I wait for you to take my key,
and shove me out the door.
Instead, you treat me
like a portrait
hanging on the wall.
Something barely
noticed, something
you acquired.

Smoke

You sit there
like you always do,
thoughts engulfed
in smoke that rises
from your cigarette.

I know you said
goodbye to her,
I saw her walk away.

Why does your shadow
dance with hers
in smoke that rises
from your cigarette?

Stench

He's a laundry bag of lies
he swears is candy.
She knows the smell is funny, but
she'd rather think he loves her,
so, she holds her nose
and smiles at what he says.
He steals her jewelry, pawns it,
then takes her on vacation,
to show he's rich
with money that is hers.
She knows that something's rotting,
but she can't find the body,
so, she sprays air freshener
everywhere she goes.
When she finds her diamonds missing,
she hits him with a shovel,
buries him, and finds the stench is gone.

Watermelons and cherries

sing sweet
serenades,
siren calls to
summer arcades,
sticky cotton
candy kisses,
photo booth
memories,
boardwalk
first crush.

What Has Passed

What has ended my desire
to do when I'm too weak, to be what I am not?
Ritual is writing through the pain.
I know that I don't know to stop until my body shatters.
The instruments of self-deception disappear
as sun-kissed skin slips into velvet darkened dress.
There is space, there is an honest sweetness in the bitter.

What secrets

do your pockets hide?
Do you keep safe
the yellowed dice,
the dog-eared cards?
What do you bet?
Eternity with God?
What last rites, what deaths
do fingers grasp?
Will you escape
the final fog of souls?

Where do you go

when the memories we cling to
crumble into stardust,
when it's hard for us
to see you in our dreams?
When all that kept you near us
is chipped away by time,
do you shadow us in sorrow,
or are you glad that now
we'll let you rest?

Wish you

would walk with me again.
Miss you. Wish you
would pull the door wide open.
Let me hold you. And tell you
over coffee how the sunlight
is a halo 'round your head.
Reconstitute. Come back.
You never liked the dark,
A grave is not the place
to hide your smile.
Miss you. Wish you
would tell me one more time
how much you miss me,
and wish me
your love.

*Inspired by "Miss you. Would like to take a walk with you."
by Gabrielle Calvocoressi*

U-Turn

You can legally U-turn
on the Main Street bridge,
return to chase your heart
across the miles,
speed-grieve under lampposts
sprouting swaying flower baskets,
watch twilight's neckline plunge
into lace camisoles of mist,
re-boil those hard
boiled eggs you couldn't peel,
return to hope that you
can find a second chance.

Yes, I know I am dying

but don't tell me I must leave,
I must let go. You frighten me,
the one I treasure, the one
who holds my hand.
Why are you so anxious
to empty out this bed?
Let me tread water in your tears
reflecting light in the diner
where you dropped
a cherry pie on my white shirt.
Do you remember?
Let me drop into delirium
of crunching leaves
beneath our boots.
Do you remember?
Soon enough the dawn
will wrap you in a rosy
robe of sorrow. Your first day
alone without me. Do you know
I hear you whisper in my ear:
I'll always love you. Time to go.

You are a misguided

missile, target lost
or simply vanished.
you are a lost
soul aboard a bus
that wanders midnight
streets in search of
heaven or hell.

Hours and Seasons

A Little Less Enthusiasm, Please

The grass has not yet brittled brown,
but here you are, so eager,
to float and flash
your bright red dress
when temperatures are warm.
I know you're only warning
of snowy days to come,
but can you wait a few more weeks
so I can find the rake?

Bed Head

Thoughts are disheveled
and so is my hair.
Ends split for cover
hiding under blankets,
cowering from light.

Best Revenge

Who is that woman
in the mirror?
It must be my mother,
not me.

I am a much
younger version
of the woman
that I see.

I wrap myself in
robes of joy,
more tightly
in my boundaries.

With a spade
I dig a hole
and plant
my feet.

The best revenge
is to blossom.

Clouds blanket

the night sky,
put starlight to sleep,
but dreams put on
swim fins and jump
out the window
as light shatters
cloud banks,
to swim with
the mermaids
in pools of moonlight.

Cracks

Sunlight cracks the darkness open.
Grab the fading moonbeams splitting
floorboards into splinters, store them
in the sidewalk cracks between the weeds.
Toss sunflower seed shells burst between
cracked knuckles into moments split between
stray thoughts. Watch sunflowers grow.

Enthusiasm without a plan

is sections of wooden slats
erected haphazardly
through the yard,
resting against
vague hopes
of becoming a fence,
of joining hands
through trees
and the neighbor's
swimming pool,
a winding noose
to suffocate spare time,
a windmill to fight
until you sell the house.

For Ken Tomaro

Sleep escapes

running wild on the street,
until the sunshine
splits her sideways
and the fragments
are a trail into twilight.

Stay as long as you want

but pay by the hour
at the Underbelly Motel.
VACANCY is a bat
blinking at your headlights.
Your room is reserved.
The spider in the corner
grants absolution
for a bottle of gin.
Your lust lays on stained sheets
with her legs wide open.
Leave your pants on the floor
and your conscience in the fridge.

This day

should be dressed in toothpaste,
minty fresh, sparkly.
But no, this day is a clothesline
slicing the clouds,
all my dirty laundry
waving to the neighbors.

Today is a dog

with gravel in her mouth
and a bad case
of indigestion.

Tulips

I stare out the window
while my coffee cools
and my eggs run
from stale toast.

Nine tulips in my garden
are bejeweled with
melted drops
of yesterday's snow.

The wind tosses new flakes
as the sky turns off the sun.
I pray my tulips survive
another dose of cold medicine.

Visiting Hours

The moon arrives,
the same time as always.
She carries stardust
and a dog-eared romance
in her purse.
The trees reach up their arms,
bare-branch longing
for her white kiss.
She cannot grasp
wood fingers below.
Trees, without mouths,
cannot whisper love.
Her oblong light
slips away from
tree shadows, defeated,
a fool's errand
repeated again.

Watch the day bruise

into night
from sun squeeze
and cloud crush.

You Whisper

Winter trails your tail
as you blow the sun to set.
I stuff my ears with red,
red leaves, let autumn
stay a few more days –
don't make things worse
before it's time.

Totally Unserious

A crazy idea

crawled through the window,
to take a quick shower
to smell fresh and clever
before it seduced me,
before I concluded
the crazy idea was insane.

Electric Beater

She frowned the beater
'round the bowl
to meld the flour into cake.
She laid the beater in the sink.
That's when we saw
the beater wasn't electric.
She was.

Give me that secret sauce

to a heart attack,
that greasy, salty
hunk of heaven.
Oh, lowly worker,
be my savior.
Bring me a box,
a bag, a promise
of fries, of fat.
Hand me my
happiness, my hope.
I park close to
your neon church,
engine idling, bask
in the tanning bed
glow of your lights.
Secret sauce, kiss
my lips, dribble
into darkness,
baptize me.

Happiness is an elephant

sitting in the best chair,
hogging the remote.
I can only feed him peanuts
and vacuum when he
goes to the refrigerator
for a beer.

He took off his skin

and shook it out the window,
watched dandelions and cobwebs
float to the ground.
He washed it in the kitchen sink,
hung it on the clothesline
to dry in the sun.
He tsk-tsked at holes left
from sharp tongues
and rough fingernails,
sewed them closed
with an extra heartstring.
He folded it up
and laid it in the bag
of useless treasures
to be taken to Goodwill.
He pulled a thicker skin
from underneath the pillow,
shrugged it on,
and went about his day.

Hope hitches a ride

on unbathed white hair.
Wind slicks and sun flicks
float with each footfall,
the floor a dusty flashback
of unswept fields, and a race
to embrace the wind.

Life in the Bathroom

Response poem to "From the Women's Restroom" by Kaitlyn Spees

A sign above
the women's bathroom sink
tells me Water
Is Life.
In red lipstick below,
Thank You for
Using Less.
How do I use
less life?
Do I stuff
wasted hours
at work
up the tampon dispenser?

Modern-day Eve

is no temptress.
She markets in
sweats and flip-flops.
Her gray hair is showing
beneath the blond streaks,
she doesn't know
whether to hide it.
No snake needs to tell her
to reach for the apples,
she knows they're on sale this week.

My brain is stained

with caffeine. My teeth
a latte white. With
French vanilla. Syrup
dreams drifting. Lazy
flecks. To land. On
croissant hours.

Squinting

Tossed glasses on table, you squint
at your phone as you take a nude
selfie, to show me your beauty we know
I can't have. I can't see your muscles,
the curve of your chest, I just see you
can't see your beautiful

thumb.

The Incident

The sunlight was a halo
around her dyed-blond head,
her fake mink promised
jasmine-scented nights.
Lacy hanky couldn't hide
mascara rivers smudging
blood-red lips.
Ya gotta help me, please!
she wailed at the lawyer's feet.
I didn't murder anyone!
The lawyer cocked a bushy brow.
There was that little incident
with three monkeys, a goat,
and a can of lima beans.
They dropped the charges
for the monkeys and goat.

The lima beans, though,
that's another story.

You're a poet, you see

the world as a ball of
multi-colored yarn,
and you want to
be that kitten, roll
it out the door, see
where it ends, taste
it, smell it. You see
the moon as a ball of
yarn, a disco ball
that showers sparkle.
You dance barefoot
through the glass that
doesn't cut, you're
a poet without writing

a single line.

You're only crazy

if you're like
everybody.
If you strip
naked
at a party
and sit in the punch
bowl
because red
is your favorite color,
you only do
what everybody
wants to do.
But they're all wimps,
not you.